Christian, the Hugging Lion

For Gemma
—J. R. and P. P.

To the Bates clan
—A. J. B.

ACKNOWLEDGMENTS: Special thanks to my children, whose playful antics inspired my depiction of Christian—A. J. B.

SIMON & SCHUSTER BOOKS FOR YOUNG READERS
An imprint of Simon & Schuster Children's Publishing Division
1230 Avenue of the Americas, New York, New York 10020
Text copyright © 2010 by Justin Richardson and Peter Parnell
Illustrations copyright © 2010 by Amy Bates

For information about special discounts for bulk purchases, please contact
Simon & Schuster Special Sales at 1-866-506-1949 or business@simonandschuster.com.
The Simon & Schuster Speakers Bureau can bring authors to your live event.
For more information or to book an event, contact the Simon & Schuster Speakers Bureau
at 1-866-248-3049 or visit our website at www.simonspeakers.com.

Book design by Laurent Linn
The text for this book is set in Buccardi.
The illustrations for this book are rendered in watercolor, gouache, and pencil.
Manufactured in China
1209 SCP
2 4 6 8 10 9 7 5 3 1

Library of Congress Cataloging-in-Publication Data
Richardson, Justin, 1963–
Christian, the hugging lion / Justin Richardson
and Peter Parnell ; illustrated by Amy Bates.—1st ed.
p. cm.
Summary: When Ace and John find a lion cub for sale at Harrods department store,
they buy him, name him Christian, and the three live happily for a year in a London apartment.
But eventually Christian grows too big and they must let him go to live the life of a wild cat.
Based on a true story; includes an author's note.
ISBN 978-1-4169-8662-1 (hardcover)
[1. Lions as pets—Fiction. 2. Lions—Fiction. 3. London (England)—Fiction. 4. England—Fiction.
5. Kenya—Fiction.] I. Parnell, Peter. II. Bates, Amy June, ill. III. Title.
PZ7.R39495Ch 2010   [E]—dc22   2009002297

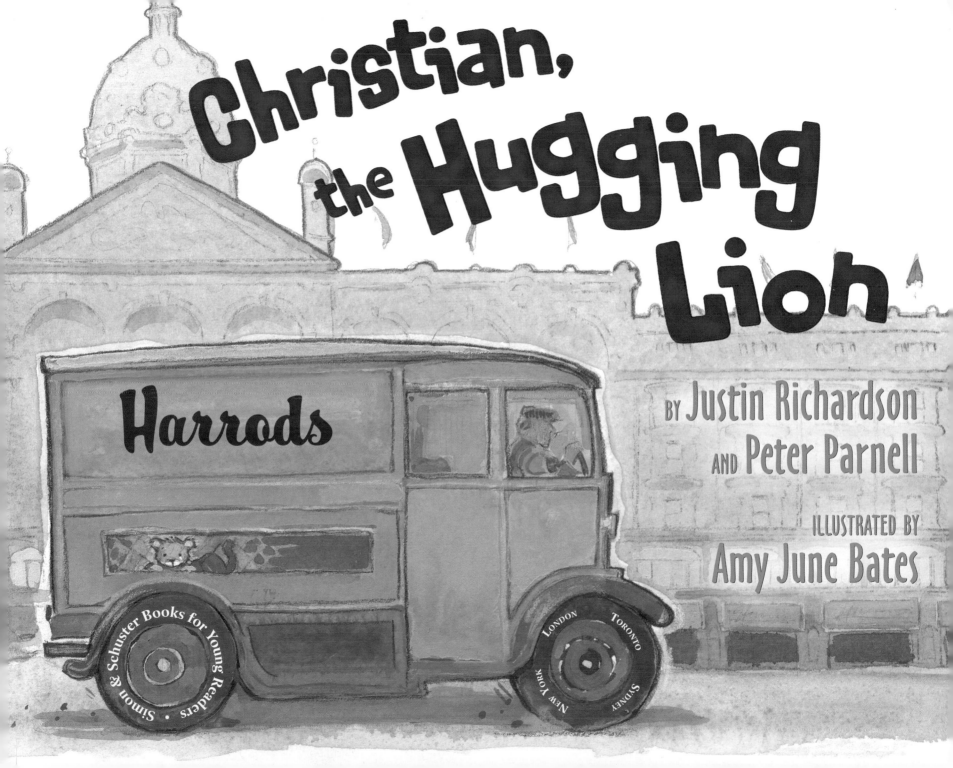

Christian, the Hugging Lion

Harrods

BY **Justin Richardson**

AND **Peter Parnell**

ILLUSTRATED BY

Amy June Bates

Many years ago, the most famous store in London made the world a promise. At Harrods you could buy absolutely anything you wanted. Anything!

What would you like? Chocolate tea? Silk pajamas? A coconut from Brazil? How about a racing car or a yacht with five white sails?

"Yessir," the clerk would say. "I'll get that right away!"

Better yet, at Harrods you could buy the most unusual pets.

"I'd like a camel, if you don't mind."

"Certainly, madam. One hump or two?"

CAMEL

One Hump . . . .
Two Humps . . . . . .
Three Humps . . . . .

One day two young men came to see what Harrods had for sale.

There, sitting in a cage beneath a honey blossom tree, was a little lion cub. He had come from the zoo.

"A store is no place for a lion to live," they said. "Something must be done!"

And so Ace and John bought him and took him back to their apartment. "We'll call him Christian," they said.

Christian curled up between his new friends on their paisley sofa. He seemed very happy to have found a home.

Christian liked to roll and play and chase his toys under the furniture. He spent hours peering through the window at the birds outside.

And he loved to put his paws on Ace's and John's shoulders and do something that wild lions never do. He hugged them.

Christian became a very well-behaved little cub.

Most of the time.

After all, he was still a lion.

Ace and John took Christian with them everywhere they went.

When they went for a stroll in the morning, they paraded him down the Kings Road.

They played with him in the churchyard.

They ate lunch with him in their favorite restaurant,
where the chef served Christian in high style.

And they even took Christian to the pub.
Christian was very friendly to everyone
he met, although sometimes his hugs were a
little clumsy.

Christian loved to take in the sights of London from the backseat of Ace and John's car. He loved to picnic at the beach on the English Channel and feel the sun on his back, although the water was disagreeably cold.

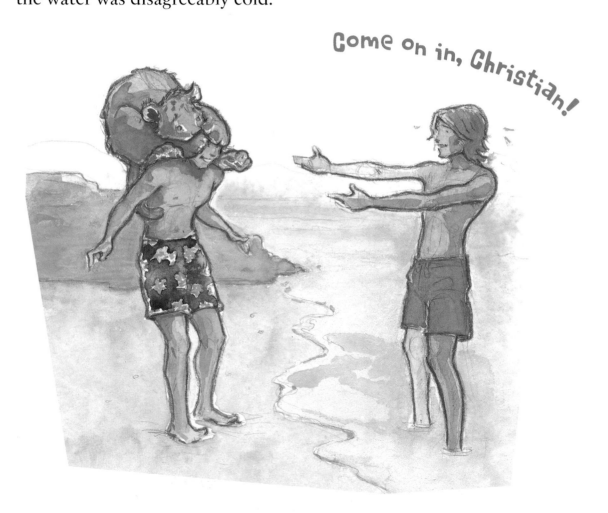

Come on in, Christian!

Most of all, Christian loved being with Ace and John. The three of them had become the most unusual family in all of London.

After a year of Christian's
eating and playing and growing,
it wasn't quite as comfortable
for Ace and John to snuggle with
him on their paisley sofa.

Should they get a bigger sofa?
Or move to a bigger apartment?
Would they have to bring
Christian to the zoo?

"No!" Ace and John decided.

"Lions belong in the wild."

Christian was happy in London, but Ace
and John knew he'd be happier in Africa.
So they made a plan to fly there.

Christian would have to travel inside a wooden crate.
He didn't seem to like the idea. Ace and John climbed in to
show him how comfortable it could be. "It's lovely in here!"

Reluctantly, Christian agreed. And every day
he practiced spending a little more time in the
crate. It was going to be a very long trip.

Finally the day came to fly.

When the three of them arrived in Kenya, a crowd gathered.

Everyone was surprised to see a lion who could ride in a plane.

"A lion from London?"

Ace and John drove Christian to meet Mr. Adamson,

who taught lions how to live in the wild. They were

worried. "How will Christian manage without

the churchyard to play in or the chef

to fix his lunch?"

"Leave him to me," Mr. Adamson said with a smile.

And so they did.

Christian looked around. The sky was wider than he had ever seen, even over Hyde Park. There were many more birds than outside his favorite window. And in the distance he saw gazelles grazing. They made his nose twitch and his hind legs feel springy.

Should he run after them? Was that allowed in Africa?

A breeze tickled Christian's fur. The air was dry and smelled of honey blossoms. It filled his chest and stirred a feeling that rattled up to his mouth and came out as a strange new sound.

Back in London, Ace and John missed Christian's hugs. They drove in their car and went on picnics and ate at their favorite restaurant. But it wasn't the same without him.

Finally, they called Mr. Adamson.

"How is Christian?" they asked.

"Very well, indeed! He's gone off into the wild."

Could they visit him?

"We could try to find him. But he may not remember you. Christian is a grown-up lion now, with cubs of his own."

"Let's go!" they said.

When they arrived in Kenya, what did they see?

Christian!

Their old friend took a long look at them.

And then . . .

They were together again! Christian and Ace and John played all day until the evening sun began to slip behind the trees. Then they settled down for a quiet night's sleep under the Kenyan stars.

Ace and John knew that in the morning Christian would go back to his new lion family. But for that night the three of them curled up together just like they used to. Cozy and snug and, of course, hugging.

Authors' Note

ALL OF THE EVENTS IN THIS STORY ARE TRUE. Christian was born to a long line of zoo lions in 1969 at the Ilfracombe Zoo in Devon, England. He was three months old when John Rendall and Ace Bourke purchased him from Harrods' exotic pet department for 250 guineas—about $4,500 in today's money.

Christian did, in fact, visit a restaurant and a pub and play ball in a churchyard. But he spent most of his days a floor or two below Ace and John's apartment in the furniture shop where they both worked. The real Christian is world-famous for his hugs. Still, hugging is not something you ought to try with just any lion.

After the reunion depicted in this book, Ace and John visited Christian one more time. By then, he had grown from a 35-pound pet cub to the 500-pound leader of a pride on the banks of the Tana River. He had become the very first member of his family in many generations to live free in Africa. During that visit Ace, John, and Christian played happily together before saying a final good-bye. The three never met again, but thanks to a now-famous video of their reunion that appeared on the Internet in 2008, their friendship lives on.